NATURAL DISASTERS

Avalanches

by Rebecca Pettiford

BELLWETHER MEDIA • MINNEAPOLIS, MN

Note to Librarians, Teachers, and Parents:

Blastoff! Readers are carefully developed by literacy experts and combine standards-based content with developmentally appropriate text.

Level 1 provides the most support through repetition of high-frequency words, light text, predictable sentence patterns, and strong visual support.

Level 2 offers early readers a bit more challenge through varied simple sentences, increased text load, and less repetition of high-frequency words.

Level 3 advances early-fluent readers toward fluency through increased text and concept load, less reliance on visuals, longer sentences, and more literary language.

Level 4 builds reading stamina by providing more text per page, increased use of punctuation, greater variation in sentence patterns, and increasingly challenging vocabulary.

Level 5 encourages children to move from "learning to read" to "reading to learn" by providing even more text, varied writing styles, and less familiar topics.

Whichever book is right for your reader, Blastoff! Readers are the perfect books to build confidence and encourage a love of reading that will last a lifetime!

This edition first published in 2020 by Bellwether Media, Inc.

No part of this publication may be reproduced in whole or in part without written permission of the publisher. For information regarding permission, write to Bellwether Media, Inc., Attention: Permissions Department, 6012 Blue Circle Drive, Minnetonka, MN 55343.

Library of Congress Cataloging-in-Publication Data

LC record for Avalanches available at https://lccn.loc.gov/2019028412

Text copyright © 2020 by Bellwether Media, Inc. BLASTOFF! READERS and associated logos are trademarks and/or registered trademarks of Bellwether Media, Inc.

Editor: Rebecca Sabelko   Designer: Josh Brink

Printed in the United States of America, North Mankato, MN

Table of Contents

What Are Avalanches?

Avalanches are fast-moving masses of ice, snow, and rock. These disasters occur on snowy mountain slopes.

They can reach speeds
of more than 80 miles
(129 kilometers) per hour!

Avalanche Danger Zones

N

W E

S

avalanche danger zone =

How Do Avalanches Form?

snowpack

Avalanches form when a **trigger** moves weak layers in the **snowpack**. Triggers can be snow, wind, or rain. They can even be **earthquakes**!

The movements of skiers and animals can also cause avalanches.

How Avalanches Form

sluff avalanche   trigger

powder snow

slab avalanche   trigger

melting snow

Sometimes the top layer of the snowpack is weak. This can cause small **sluff avalanches**.

sluff avalanche

Sluff avalanches are made of powdery snow. They do not cause much damage.

Slab avalanches are more dangerous. Rising **temperatures** melt top layers of snow.

slab avalanche

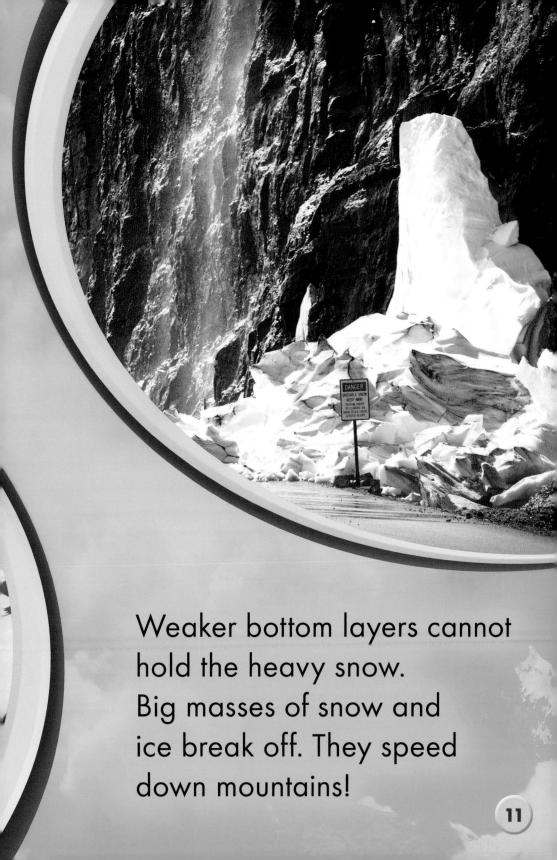

Weaker bottom layers cannot hold the heavy snow. Big masses of snow and ice break off. They speed down mountains!

Avalanches can block roads and destroy buildings.

Blocked roads keep emergency vehicles from passing. They keep people from getting to work or school.

Avalanches can destroy **habitats**.

But they can also help create new ones! New plant and animal homes grow from the damage.

Avalanche Danger Scale

Danger Level	Warnings
Extreme:	• stay away from all avalanche areas
High:	• very dangerous
Major:	• dangerous
Minor:	• avalanches possible
Low:	• few avalanches possible

Predicting Disaster

Most avalanches happen from December to April. Scientists can usually **predict** when they will happen.

They study past avalanches. They use **radar** to track weather. Cameras help them spot movements in the snowpack.

radar

Scientists may use **explosives** to start small avalanches. This can stop more dangerous ones from forming.

They also put up fences. These stop snow from reaching buildings and towns.

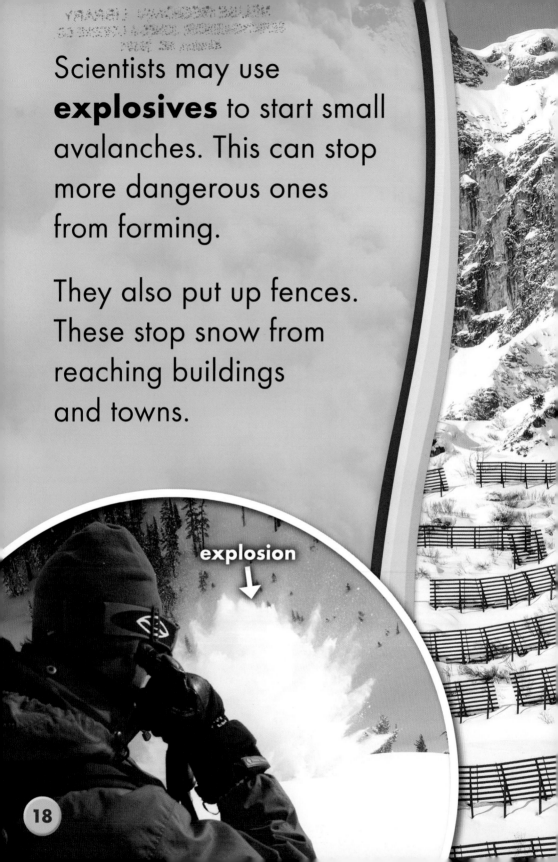

explosion

Avalanche Profile

Name:	The Yungay Avalanche
Date:	May 31, 1970
Location:	Yungay, Peru
Damage to Property:	Yungay destroyed
Damage to People:	at least 17,000 people lost lives

It is smart to stay informed.
Always check for
avalanche **warnings**.

Keep away from slopes with a lot of snowfall. Avalanches can be triggered at any time!

Glossary

earthquakes—events in which the earth's surface shakes that often cause a lot of damage

explosives—substances used to blow something up

habitats—the natural homes of plants and animals

predict—to use information to guess what may happen

radar—a system that measures direction, distance, and speed; radar can track storms.

slab avalanches—large avalanches that are made of blocks of snow and ice

sluff avalanches—small avalanches that are made of powdery snow

snowpack—a mass of snow on the ground that is solid and hard

temperatures—how cold or hot things are

trigger—something that causes something else to happen

warnings—alerts issued by meteorologists when avalanches, or signs of avalanches, have been spotted in an area

To Learn More

AT THE LIBRARY

Maurer, Tracy Nelson. *World's Worst Avalanches*. North Mankato, Minn.: Capstone Press, 2019.

Otfinoski, Steven. *Avalanches*. New York, N.Y.: Children's Press, 2016.

Rusch, Elizabeth. *Avalanche Dog Heroes: Piper and Friends Learn to Search the Snow*. Seattle, Wash.: Little Bigfoot, 2018.

ON THE WEB

FACTSURFER

Factsurfer.com gives you a safe, fun way to find more information.

1. Go to www.factsurfer.com.

2. Enter "avalanches" into the search box and click 🔍.

3. Select your book cover to see a list of related web sites.

Index